I0820241

CREATIVE CAREERS

Creative Careers in the

CULINARY ARTS

Stuart A. Kallen

San Diego, CA

For more information, contact:
ReferencePoint Press, Inc.
PO Box 27779
San Diego, CA 92198
www.ReferencePointPress.com

LIBRARY OF CONGRESS CATALOGING-IN-PUBLICATION DATA

Author: Stuart A. Kallen
Title: Creative Careers in the Culinary Arts
Description: San Diego, CA : ReferencePoint Press, 2026. | Series: Creative Careers
Includes bibliographical references and index
Identifiers: LCCN 2025012580 (print) | ISBN 9781678210229 library binding | ISBN 9781678210236 ebook

For compete cataloging-in-publication data please go to www.loc.gov.

Contents

Introduction: The Art of Cooking 4

Pastry Chef 6

Sushi Chef 14

Chocolatier 22

Executive Chef 30

Food Stylist 38

Craft Brewer 46

Source Notes 54
Interview with a Sushi Chef 57
Other Jobs in the Culinary Arts 59
Index 60
Picture Credits 64
About the Author 64

Introduction: The Art of Cooking

During his thirty-plus years as an award-winning executive chef, Lee Hillson has cooked for presidents, royals, celebrities, and rock stars. Hillson competed in the Food Network's *Iron Chef America* reality television (TV) show and has run some of the most prestigious kitchens in the United States. Born in London, Hillson spent part of his childhood in Australia, where his parents hosted large cookouts for friends nearly every weekend. After watching a family friend cook jumbo shrimp on a barbeque, Hillson decided on his future career. As Hillson recalled in 2022, "I remember the first thing I ever made. I took flour and water, mixed it together and made a dough, put ketchup on it and some cheese. Made a pizza."[1] He was six years old.

The family moved back to London, where Hillson attended culinary school at age sixteen. After taking courses for more than two years and training as a pastry chef, Hillson interned at the upscale restaurant at London's esteemed Four Seasons Hotel. He gained more experience cooking at London's famed—but now closed—Le Gavroche, which served French cuisine. Hillson then moved to Phoenix, Arizona, where he worked as a sous chef, or second in command, in a resort kitchen. There, he learned to cook for many guests at once, serving up gourmet meals at banquets. He worked at various other resorts before taking on the role of executive chef at the chic Phoenician Resort in Scottsdale. In 2025 Hillson continued to develop menus and manage dozens of employees as executive chef of the T. Cook's restaurant at the Royal Palms Resort in Phoenix.

Hillson's story reveals how a love of cooking, coupled with hard work and a culinary education, can lead to a long, successful career as an executive chef. Hillson says that creatively prepared food does more than fill the belly. The flavors and aromas can help people remember happy moments from their lives. A recollection might include a fantastic vacation or a meal prepared long ago by a grandmother: "What we do as chefs is we evoke memories. . . . That's what food is about. That's what we do. We just make people's memories."[2]

An Attainable but Demanding Job

Culinary artists like Hillson are in great demand. The Bureau of Labor Statistics (BLS) says that the job market for executive chefs and other food specialists will grow by 15 percent by 2031. And while some chefs train at prestigious cooking institutes in other countries, students on a budget can obtain a two-year associate's degree in culinary arts for around half the cost of a bachelor's degree at an average university.

As any experienced culinary artist will tell you, working in a commercial kitchen is not easy. Chefs and other restaurant personnel almost always work nights, holidays, and weekends. Kitchens are hot, floors are slippery, and there is a constant risk of cuts and burns. During peak hours, the job can be stressful. But as a chef known online as Bentley says, "When you can work alongside other people . . . and you can create a beautifully synchronized performance, it makes it all worth it."[3]

With the hospitality and tourism sector growing at a rapid pace, those who understand kitchen dynamics, cooking techniques, food science, dining trends, and plating aesthetics can have creative careers that pay well. Culinary artists can find work in almost every city in the country, and some go on to start their own eateries, online businesses, catering companies, and restaurant consulting firms. According to dietary consultant James Constantine Frangos, "The culinary arts field is like a big, delicious pie, with each slice representing a different career path. There are many roles to consider. . . . Each role requires unique skills and offers its own tasty opportunities for growth and specialization."[4]

What Does a Pastry Chef Do?

"Dessert is the finishing note in the symphony of a meal," says Leni Rose Magsino. "There has to be a sweet note to finish the experience."[5] There is a good reason Magsino compares dessert to a musical crescendo. She is a Florida-based pastry chef who turns humdrum ingredients like sugar, flour, and eggs into delectable treats that bring smiles to her customers.

At a Glance

Number of Jobs
243,400*

Pay
$68,816 in 2025

Educational Requirements
Associate's degree in baking and the pastry arts

Personal Qualities
Creative, attention to detail, good communicator, hard worker

Working Conditions
Full-time in kitchens, which can be hot, loud, and stressful

Future Job Outlook
Growth of 5 percent through 2033*

* For all bakers

Pastry chefs like Magsino say that their vocation involves both art and science. The chefs use their artistic flair to create a wide range of pastries, desserts, breads, and baked goods that are as pleasing to the eye as they are to the taste buds. Pastry chefs often take artistic inspiration from nature, sculpture, and classical artwork. Pastry chef Pierre Hermé is often referred to as "the Picasso of Pastry" because his stunning dessert designs are reminiscent of the unique artworks created by the iconic artist Pablo Picasso. Hermé describes his creative process: "I start off with an idea, ingredient, or emotion, and I compose something in my head. Then I transpose that on paper [into] a recipe. And that is turned into a sketch, because I want to see the proportions and what the architecture of the flavors can be."[6] When the initial work is done, Hermé turns the recipe over to a team of chefs who work on bringing the creation to life. They determine how much of each ingredient to use and ensure that the finished product lives up to the standards determined by Hermé.

Pastry chefs like Hermé spend their days researching new recipes. They page through magazines and scroll through digital articles for inspiration. The chefs experiment with new and unusual ingredients that might include herbs, spices, alcoholic beverages, and even edible flowers. Whatever the ingredients, pastry chefs understand there is little room for error. Dinner chefs can make minor mistakes like not adding enough salt or having a flame a little too high under a frying pan. But as pastry chef Precious Pioneer writes, "Pastry chefs must have strong attention to detail to ensure their desserts are consistently high quality. Making excellent pastries involves precise measurements, careful temperature control, and precise timing."[7]

Pastry chefs have different specialties. Executive pastry chefs are those with the most experience. They are responsible for creating a dining establishment's dessert menu. During this process they work with wine stewards to determine which after-dinner wines and other dessert beverages are best paired with pastries. Cake designers focus on baking and decorating cakes, which involves developing cake components, including fillings, syrups, and icing. Cake designers need strong artistic skills to decorate cakes with intricate, highly detailed designs. Frozen dessert specialists create ice cream, gelato, and sorbet, and confectioners make candies, caramels, and other sugary treats. Some pastry chefs meet the demand for healthier foods by specializing in vegan and low-sugar desserts.

In addition to baking, pastry chefs manage ingredient inventories to ensure they have high-quality items for their recipes.

Additionally, pastry chefs train and supervise other cooks, bakers, and assistants. And they need to maintain hygienic workspaces and follow strict food safety and sanitation standards to prevent foodborne illnesses.

How Do You Become a Pastry Chef?

Education and Training

Most pastry chefs have at least a two-year associate's degree in baking and the pastry arts. But some great pastry chefs say they were born to bake. That is certainly the case with Collette Christian. She took a high school baking course at age fourteen and fell in love with the process. A month later Christian landed her first baking job at a Chicago restaurant, where she received on-the-job training. Christian went on to perfect her pastry baking skills at some of the finest dining establishments in the country. "I've worked in some real fairytale kitchens," she says. "Five star hotels, really beautiful restaurants. And then I also worked in some great small places."[8]

Christian started her own restaurant and wedding cake business when she was in her late twenties. But even with her years of experience, she still wanted to obtain a formal education. She took online courses from the Auguste Escoffier School of Culinary Arts and graduated with an associate's degree. While it might seem unusual to learn to bake online, students attend live classes led by professional chefs. They have access to hundreds of recipes, step-by-step baking videos, and other materials, and they work in their own kitchens, where they document their progress. The school tool kit includes a uniform, chef's knives, and pastry-making supplies.

Christian, who was the mother of a small child when she attended school, says that online courses were perfect for her because she did not have to arrange child care. Those who want more hands-on experience can earn an associate's degree in

Join a Bakery Club

"Seek out local business associations or bakery clubs in your area where fellow bakers and pastry enthusiasts gather to share ideas, tips, and, most importantly, support. These groups are great for exchanging knowledge, discovering local trends, and even swapping recipes. . . . Soon enough, you'll be deep in conversations about gluten-free challenges, sourdough starters that just won't cooperate, and even those unforgettable delivery disasters we all secretly love to share. . . . Joining a bakery club is about more than just networking—it's about building friendships and a support system that can make your journey as a [pastry chef] a lot more fun and rewarding."

—Cyd Mitchell Hodges, bakery consultant

Cyd Mitchell Hodges, "Kneading Connections: Building a Bakery Community Through Networking," Retail Bakers of America, October 3, 2024. www.retailbakersofamerica.org.

baking and the pastry arts at community colleges or at schools such as the Culinary Institute of America, which has campuses in California, New York, and Texas. Culinary students study pastry techniques, ingredients and baking technology, and business skills. Some obtain bachelor's degrees in the pastry arts. Courses include food science, menu management, and regulations and laws that govern the hospitality industry.

Internships

Most students who take culinary classes in the pastry arts work as interns before or immediately after graduation. Internships, which usually last around three months, provide hands-on experience for students, who learn what it is like to work in a professional kitchen. Describing how her internship at the Wild Leaven Bakery in Taos, New Mexico, exceeded her expectations, pastry chef Katie Medina says, "I have gained so much knowledge about what

A pastry chef squeezes éclair dough from a pastry bag. Blending art and science, pastry chefs transform sugar, flour, eggs, and other ingredients into delectable pastries, desserts, and breads.

it takes to either run a bakery or be employed as a professional baker. Everyone around me provided so much support and gave me clear instructions throughout my work experience. The entire work experience at Wild Leaven Bakery has made me more confident in the skills that I have already acquired."[9]

Certification

Pastry chefs who wish to stand out with employers and demonstrate their commitment to their craft can obtain accreditation from the American Culinary Federation. There are several levels of certification, including certified baker, certified decorator, certified executive pastry chef, and certified master pastry chef. Candidates with prior education and work experience complete classes online, including thirty hours of sanitation coursework. A two-day exam must be completed and, depending on the certification level, candidates might also be judged on their kitchen skills, presentation, and mastery of various types of pastry.

Skills and Personality

Pastry chefs rely on a combination of artistic talent, baking skills, and physical stamina. They know how to accurately measure and mix ingredients and bake them at the proper temperature for the right amount of time. Pastry chefs need to understand how to create custard, caramelize sugar, decorate cakes, and bake bread. They have good knife skills for slicing and plating desserts, and they know how to present food in an artistic manner.

Professional kitchens are often busy, hot, and loud, and pastry chefs need a range of skills to create delicious desserts in a high-pressure environment. Attention to detail is necessary to precisely measure and mix ingredients. Good communication skills are required to work in harmony with executive chefs and other less-skilled kitchen staff. Pastry chefs need to be highly organized to manage multiple recipes and ingredient inventories. And the ability to handle stress is important when things go wrong, which they often do.

On the Job

Employers

Pastry chefs work in restaurants, large hotels, bakeries, and cafés. Some work on cruise ships. Those who are employed at larger restaurants might oversee the establishment's entire dessert program.

Working Conditions

Pastry chefs often begin their day when the rest of the city is sleeping. Those employed by bakeries and breakfast establishments are often hard at work by 5:00 a.m. Chefs who make pastries for dessert shops or dinner restaurants might have more normal schedules.

I Love Being a Pastry Chef

"Every day as a pastry chef brings a new opportunity for me to unleash my creativity and breathe life into my visions. The joy of combining simple ingredients like flour and sugar to create stunning and mouthwatering treats is incomparable. . . . The artistry involved in pastry work leaves room for endless exploration. Whether it's meticulously piping intricate designs on a cake, delicately assembling layers of a dessert, or harmonizing flavors in a perfect balance, the possibilities are limitless. I relish the freedom to experiment, infusing unique flavors, textures, and visual elements to create remarkable desserts that engage all the senses."

—Baker B, vegan pastry chef

Baker B, "A Passionate Journey: Why I Love Being a Pastry Chef," Medium, October 23, 2023. https://medium.com.

Pastry chefs who work in restaurants usually prepare desserts in advance, and they rarely work alone. Some are part of a pastry team that includes individuals who focus on a single specialty like fruit sauces, chilled desserts, breads, or cakes. By the time diners are being seated in an upscale restaurant, the pastry chef is done for the day. When desserts are ordered, they are plated by a chef called a garde-manger, which is French for "pantry chef."

Earnings and Advancement

The BLS has a category for bakers but does not have a separate listing for pastry chefs. According to the BLS, the mean annual salary for all bakers was $34,950 in 2023. However, average bakers do not have the training or skills of pastry chefs, who can earn considerably more. The job evaluation site Salary.com says pastry chefs earned an average of $68,816 in 2025. Those with the most skills and experience earned over $78,000.

What Is the Future Outlook for Pastry Chefs?

The BLS says that the job outlook for all bakers is expected to grow by 5 percent through 2033. But as more diners demand tasty, healthful desserts, demand for pastry chefs is expected to grow faster.

Find Out More

American Culinary Federation (ACF)

www.acfchefs.org

The ACF offers educational courses at all levels, from student to professional. The federation is best known for its industry standard accreditation commission, which offers certification programs for pastry chefs, sous chefs, executive chefs, and others.

Pastry Chefs of America

https://pastrychefsofamerica.org

The mission of the Pastry Chefs of America is to provide education and support to pastry professionals. The website features blogs, news, classified ads, and a library, along with photos and videos of desserts and baked goods.

Retail Bakers of America

www.retailbakersofamerica.org

This organization supports and promotes the baking industry. The website has a certification program, a career center, business blogs, bakery startup guides, and other industry resources.

What Does a Sushi Chef Do?

In Japanese, the word *sushi* simply means "sour rice" or "vinegar rice." While sushi rice provides a foundation for most dishes, the Japanese cuisine known as sushi embodies much more. The style of food associated with the term *sushi* originated in Tokyo in the early nineteenth century and combines fish and other seafood with ingredients like vegetables, fruits, eggs, and seaweed. Often, these elements are used to make raw fish dishes the Japanese call sashimi. However, when small cakes of sushi rice are topped with fish or other types of seafood, the Japanese refer to these as *nigiri*. Similarly, rice with various fillings wrapped in seaweed is called *maki*. Despite the distinct naming, many people—especially outside of Japan—commonly refer to them collectively as varieties of sushi.

Sashimi, nigiri, maki, and a variety of other seafood and rice dishes are created by master sushi chefs, traditionally referred to as *itamae* (ita-meh-ee) in Japanese. Sushi chefs appreciate the rich cultural traditions of sushi and the artistry required to prepare it properly. While other chefs work in kitchens out of the public eye,

At a Glance

Number of Jobs
17,846 in 2025

Pay
$43,000 in 2025

Educational Requirements
None, but apprenticeship is usually required

Personal Qualities
Good communicator, cutlery skills, knowledge of Japanese cuisine

Working Conditions
Full-time, fast paced, long hours

Future Job Outlook
Growth of 15 percent through 2028

sushi masters often act as performing chefs striving to create memorable dining experiences. The chefs stand behind counters that face the public. As customers enter a restaurant, the sushi chef will often shout out the Japanese word for welcome (*irasshaimase*). When serving the diners, the sushi chefs will dramatically slice raw fish or vegetables into perfect strips, skillfully combine them with other ingredients, and serve the dishes with a flourish. This is done with grace and precision while wielding razor-sharp knives, called *hocho*.

Each type of hocho is designed for a specific task. The *yanagiba*, which roughly translates to willow-leaf blade, is long and thin and is used to slice fish without ripping or tearing the flesh. The *fuguhiki* is even thinner and is used to cut extremely fine slices of fish. The *takohiki* has a square end and is commonly used to lift and transfer fish slices from cutting boards to serving plates. The *oroshi* hocho is a long blade—up to 60 inches (150 cm)—used to cut large ocean fish such as tuna. Hocho can cost more than $1,500 each, so chefs care for them. Many sharpen their knives several times a day using whetstones to maintain fine edges.

Raw fish spoils quickly and can sicken customers if not handled properly. Sushi chefs use their expertise to choose the freshest fish at fish markets that open before sunrise. As sushi chef Warren Ransom writes,

> At the market, the chef carefully examines each fish. Freshness is key, so they look for clear eyes, firm flesh, and a bright, shiny appearance. The chef might also consider the season and the best catch of the day. This process is crucial because the quality of the fish directly impacts the flavor and safety of the sushi, and ensures the cleanliness of the food. . . . Samples are inspected, tasted, and the day truly begins.[10]

Rice Is the Sushi Heartbeat

"The preparation of sushi rice is a meticulous and almost ritualistic process. The rice is rinsed several times to remove excess starch, then cooked to perfection. After cooking, it is seasoned with a precise mixture of rice vinegar, sugar, and salt. The chef carefully folds the rice to ensure even seasoning and to maintain its delicate texture. . . . The vinegar mixture must enhance the flavor of the rice without overpowering the taste of the fish. The chef's experience and palate are crucial in achieving the right balance. This attention to detail ensures that the rice complements the fish, creating a harmonious bite."

—Warren Ransom, sushi chef

Warren Ransom, "A Day in the Life of a Sushi Chef," SushiFAQ.com, June 26, 2024. www.sushifaq.com.

Some sushi chefs work to promote healthier oceans by patronizing suppliers that support sustainable fishing practices. Once the supply of fish is purchased, sushi chefs are responsible for maintaining high standards of sanitation to avoid contamination from bacteria on countertops, knives, and other items.

In addition to creating delicious artistic dishes, sushi chefs have administrative tasks. They oversee restaurant finances and monitor and maintain inventory to ensure food supplies are adequate. Sushi chefs hire and fire restaurant personnel and train apprentices.

How Do You Become a Sushi Chef?

Education and Training

No college degree is required to become a sushi chef, but, in the Japanese tradition, apprentices called *deshi* work for several years to become sushi chefs. The task requires devotion and discipline. Most deshi start out as kitchen apprentices who perform mundane tasks like scrubbing pots and pans and cleaning the restaurant and kitchen. As Japanese culture expert Kevin Kilcoyne writes, "The purpose of this is to show one's devotion to becoming an *itamae*. By knuckling down, doing one's best, never complaining, and being an indispensable part of the team, a *deshi* might be given the most integral task of the sushi making process: preparing the rice."[11]

Making sushi rice with salt, sugar, and vinegar might sound easy, but only properly prepared rice can provide the crucial textures and flavors needed for high-quality sushi. As sushi chef Yoshio Sakuta says, "I believe the rice is more important than the fish itself, because it determines how much flavor the fish brings out in the sushi."[12] There are many different types of sushi rice and vinegar blends, and rice making is considered sacred by some. Sushi chefs rely on secret rice recipes that might have been developed for years or even handed down for generations. Those who are trusted in this position must unfailingly make high-quality rice on a regular basis.

Becoming *wakita* is the next step toward sushi chef. *Wakita* means "close to the chopping board." Apprentices might work for an extended time in this position. Wakita help the sushi chef by grating ginger, cutting vegetables, and preparing wasabi, a pungent horseradish condiment used on sushi. As wakita advance in training, they learn to slice up fish and prepare it by frying or marinating. Those who continue up the career ladder are allowed to handle their own professional sushi knives. This is seen as a major accomplishment, and once this role is completed, wakita can move on to become master sushi chefs. At this point they are qualified to open their own restaurants.

The traditional path to becoming a master sushi chef can take a decade. But there are numerous sushi chef institutes in the United States that provide students with intensive training programs that last for months rather than years. Courses cover basic cooking methods, ingredients, popular dishes, sushi rice preparation, and knife techniques. These culinary schools also offer classes in catering, sushi restaurant management, and other aspects of the industry. These quick courses provide a foundation for those who might want to prepare prepackaged sushi for grocery stores. But those who wish to become master sushi chefs will still need to work as apprentices in most cases.

Certification

Sushi chefs are not required to be certified, but such credentials provide evidence of their skills and knowledge. The Master of Japanese Cuisine Academy is one of the online culinary institutes that offer sushi chef education and certification. The curriculum for certification covers topics such as rice preparation, various fish slicing methods, proper fish storage, and sushi-making techniques.

Some states, such as California, require all restaurant managers to take an accredited food safety certification program every five years. The National Restaurant Association offers the industry standard ServSafe training and certification programs, including the ServSafe Food Handler certification, which is available to all food service employees.

Skills and Personality

Sushi chefs need excellent communication skills to greet customers, instruct apprentices, and direct kitchen staff. Business acumen is necessary for those who own or manage restaurants. A high degree of professionalism is also required to negotiate with fish suppliers and gain access to the highest-quality ingredients. As Ransom writes, "This relationship [with suppliers] is built on trust, mutual respect, and a shared commitment to quality. Plus, it makes for good business."[13]

Sushi chefs need to be meticulous when it comes to cleaning and sterilizing cutting boards, knives, and other equipment. And as with any restaurant professional, sushi chefs need to be hard

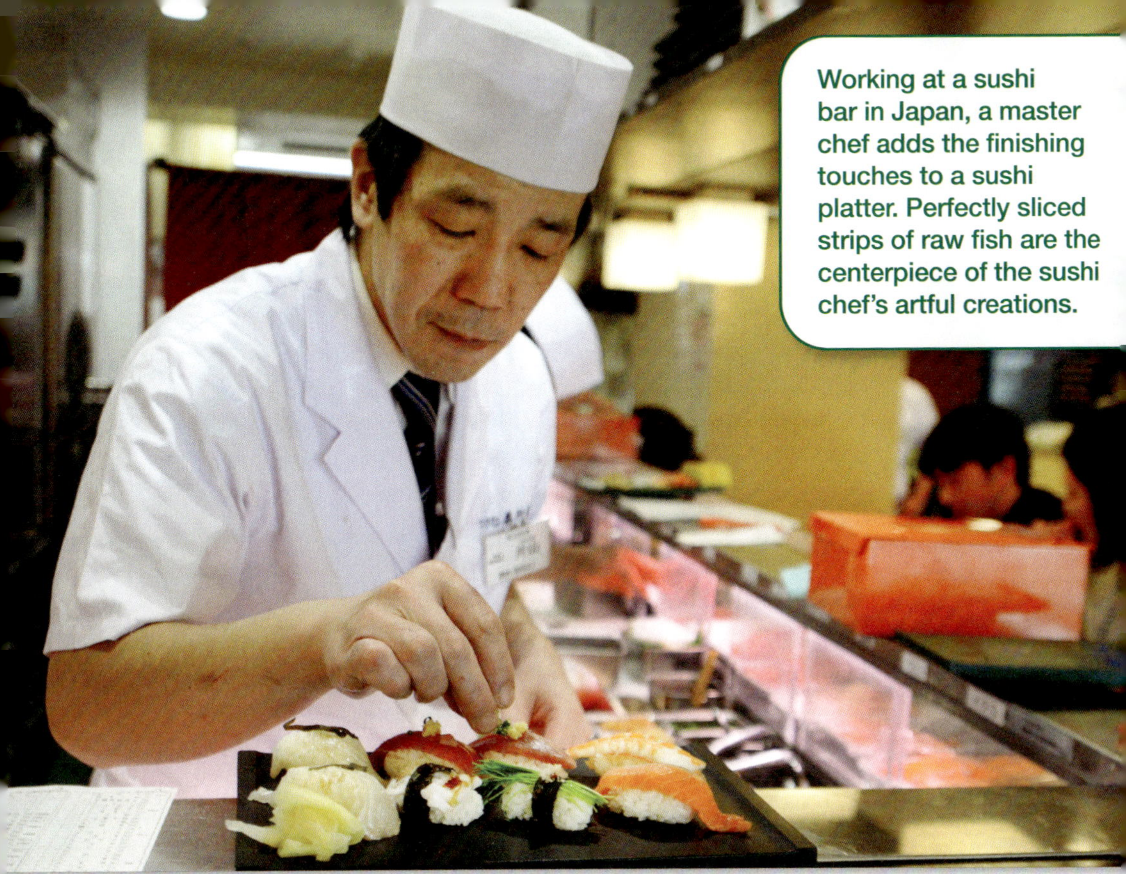

Working at a sushi bar in Japan, a master chef adds the finishing touches to a sushi platter. Perfectly sliced strips of raw fish are the centerpiece of the sushi chef's artful creations.

workers who are dedicated to their art. As Tokyo sushi master Jiro Ono says, "Once you decide on your occupation [as a sushi chef], you must immerse yourself in your work. You have to fall in love with your work. Never complain about your job. You must dedicate your life to mastering your skill. That's the secret of success and is the key to being regarded honorably."[14]

On the Job

Employers

Most sushi chefs work at Japanese eateries that range from chain restaurants such as Benihana to independently own establishments referred to as sushi bars. Sushi chefs also find employment at major facilities, such as Fuji Food Products (FFP) and Advanced Fresh Concepts. These large companies prepare and ship premade sushi to grocery stores, convenience marts, and other outlets in all

The Importance of Knife Skills

"The meticulous art of fish slicing is paramount in the world of sushi, demanding razor-sharp precision and an unwavering hand. A sushi chef's blade must glide effortlessly through the delicate flesh, ensuring clean, smooth cuts that preserve the integrity of the fish's texture and flavor. . . . In the realm of sushi, the knife is not merely a tool but an extension of the chef's artistry. Through honed knife skills, a sushi chef can elevate the dining experience, creating masterpieces that delight the senses and captivate the palate with each precise slice."

—Benjamin Bragard, chief executive officer of Everyday Uniforms

Benjamin Bragard, "Ultimate Guide to Becoming a Sushi Chef," Everyday Uniforms, March 18, 2024. https://everyday-uniforms.com.

fifty states. Chefs who are sometimes seen preparing sushi for sale in supermarkets such as Trader Joe's, Sprouts, and Sam's Club often work for FFP. Sushi chefs can also find work with catering companies that provide sushi for public and private events.

Working Conditions

Any restaurant work can be exhausting, and sushi chefs work harder than most. This is especially true for those who own their own restaurants. It is not unusual for sushi chefs to be on their feet for an entire twelve-hour shift, including on weekends, nights, and holidays. Cutting up fish for hours can be messy, smelly, and grueling and is not for the squeamish. The work is fast paced, and extremely sharp knives can cause serious injuries.

Earnings and Advancement

The average annual salary for a sushi chef in 2025 was nearly $43,000 according to the career website Zippia. However, master sushi chefs, and those who own their own restaurants, can expect to earn more than $62,000 annually.

What Is the Future Outlook for Sushi Chefs?

The sushi restaurant sector was valued at nearly $28 billion in 2024, according to the statistics website Statista. This means there is a great demand for master sushi chefs. Zippia predicts demand for sushi chefs to grow by 15 percent through 2028.

Find Out More

Association for the Advancement of the Japanese Culinary Arts (AAJ)

www.nihonryori-ken.or.jp

The AAJ was founded in 1930 to share Japanese recipes and cooking skills with chefs throughout the world. The organization offers recipes, cooking tutorials, a recipe search engine, and a resource directory in several languages.

Master of Japanese Cuisine Academy

www.master-jpcuisine.com

This culinary academy provides online courses approved by the World Association of Chef Societies global network. The school offers a free trial master class for preparation of sushi, sashimi, and other Japanese dishes.

Sushi Chef Institute (SCI)

https://sushischool.net

The SCI offers courses in sushi making and Japanese cooking techniques. The school helps students qualify for internships in Japan and offers job support and other services to graduates.

What Does a Chocolatier Do?

Katrina Markoff owns three boutiques, runs a successful e-commerce platform, and travels the world studying food cultures on nearly every continent. Markoff powers her lifestyle by making and selling one of the world's best-loved foods: chocolate. As an artisan chocolatier, Markoff expertly combines sugar, milk, and cocoa beans, which grow on cacao trees. But Markoff's chocolates could not be more different from those found on the shelves of grocery stores. She adds exotic ingredients such as spicy curry from India, smoky paprika from Hungary, and pungent wasabi horseradish from Japan.

As the founder and chief executive officer of Vosges Chocolat, Markoff is one of the most successful chocolatiers in the world. She sells her unique treats for fifty to one hundred dollars per box. And Markoff says she hopes to provide more than unique taste treats to her customers: "When I first started creating these chocolates with ingredients from all over the world . . . I was like, 'Wow! This is bringing all the world's cultures into one box in such a harmonious,

At a Glance

Number of Jobs
48,000 in 2025

Pay
$43,981 in 2025

Educational Requirements
Associate's degree recommended

Personal Qualities
Artistic, discerning palate, physical dexterity, good business skills

Working Conditions
Full-time with some overtime, stressful kitchen work

Future Job Outlook
Growth of 6 percent through 2034

symbiotic way. Can [we] bring more peace to the world through chocolate?'"[15]

Most chocolatiers recognize that sweets are significant sources of fats and sugars, but they also understand that chocolate, when eaten in moderation, can have health benefits. Cocoa beans contain substances called flavonoids that improve heart health and reduce inflammation. Research shows that chocolate causes the brain to release chemicals like endorphins and dopamine that boost feelings of pleasure. This is why chocolatier Estelle Tracy says, "I'm in the joy business."[16]

Chocolatiers are expert chefs who create confections that taste fantastic and have great visual appeal. They use their cooking skills to create handmade truffles, bonbons, tarts, cakes, bars, pastries, and chocolate sculptures. Chocolatiers might include fillings like fruits, nuts, spices, and liqueurs and add detailed decorations to their treats.

They use a variety of techniques in their work. Chocolatiers fill molds with liquid chocolate to create treats that are similar in size and shape. They are masters of techniques such as tempering, which involves heating and cooling chocolate to achieve a shiny texture. And chocolatiers use their artistic skills to make attention-grabbing chocolate sculptures for events and festivals.

Chocolatiers have a good understanding of all varieties of chocolate and know which type to use for best results. For example, dark chocolate has an intense, bittersweet flavor because it is at minimum 35 percent cocoa, which has an acidic flavor. This type of chocolate is ideal for truffles. Milk chocolate, used for candies, is creamy because it has a high percentage of milkfat, the natural fat found in milk. White chocolate, used for pastry fillings and wafers, retains its color because it is made with cocoa butter, a semisolid, whitish fat extracted from cocoa beans.

According to Ecole Chocolat Professional School of Chocolate Arts, around 3 percent of chocolate makers can be categorized as artisan chocolatiers. Some refer to themselves as bean-to-bar makers. They are involved in every step of the chocolate-making process. Mark Schimmel, owner of Krak Chocolade, explains why he is in the bean-to-bar business: “Bean-to-bar chocolate tends to be more sustainable and ethical compared to mass-produced variants. Chocolate makers who follow this process often source their cocoa beans directly from farmers, ensuring fair prices and decent work conditions. Plus, we have the choice to use only top-quality, sustainably sourced cocoa beans.”[17] Bean-to-bar chocolatiers usually sell their products in their own boutiques and online. Some sell their goods at a discount to prominent retailers, specialty food stores, and chocolate resellers.

In addition to making great chocolate delicacies, chocolatiers like Markoff focus on business and administrative tasks. They talk, text, and email with customers, suppliers, and employees; perform accounting tasks; and oversee payrolls. Food-based businesses are also required to follow strict government sanitation and food-safety standards.

How Do You Become a Chocolatier?

Education and Training

A college degree is not necessary for those who wish to create gourmet chocolates, but most chocolatiers possess an associate's degree in culinary arts. Describing her path to becoming a chocolatier, Rachel McKinley recalls,

> I was a student headed towards a career in medicine. . . . I loved baking, though, especially with chocolate, so I made time to experiment with infusions and flavors and make beautiful, tasty desserts for my friends. . . . I got the idea to sell truffles as a side gig to friends and friends-of-friends to make a bit of cash. I figured I'd sell maybe 300 truffles for $1 each. I ended up making and selling 3,000 truffles.[18]

Bringing Joy with Science and Art

"Before I got into the chocolate world, I studied Biochemistry and Microbiology, and I have a deep understanding and interest in ingredients and how they work together. That led to my desire to be a Research and Development Chocolatier and to focus on the creation of new things. . . . I love, love, love going into our shops and seeing people get excited about products that I've created. I became a Chocolatier because I realized how much I like it from . . . a science and creative perspective, but I also realized how much joy it brought people. Seeing that happen . . . is the pinnacle of my job."

—Rachel McKinley, chocolatier

Quoted in Canadian Manufacturers & Exporters, "Herstory: Rachel McKinley." https://cme-mec.ca.

McKinley says making truffles proved to be more satisfying and more fun than studying medicine. And the processes allowed her to combine her scientific background with her creative impulses. McKinley signed up for an online course from Ecole Chocolat and earned a degree.

Whether students pursue their degrees online or in a classroom, culinary lessons provide vital knowledge. Student chocolatiers learn to develop recipes; master manufacturing processes; and dip, mold, decorate, and sculpt chocolate like professionals. Most culinary institutes also teach business skills like pricing, brand building, accounting, inventory management, and customer service.

Those who wish to continue their education can pursue a bachelor's degree in a culinary school. In-person or online courses further crafting skills but also emphasize the managerial and entrepreneurial sides of the industry. There are even scholarships for students to study abroad in European culinary schools.

A chocolatier squeezes medallions of luscious chocolate from a pastry bag. Chocolatiers work with different types of chocolate and fillings to create confections such as truffles, bonbons, tarts, and cakes.

Internships

After McKinley completed her online chocolatier courses, she took on an internship at the Chocolate Academy, which offers on-location live master classes in New York City. She was mentored by master chocolatier Julian Rose and went on to join the faculty of her online alma mater, Ecole Chocolat. McKinley went on to open two chocolate boutiques in Quebec, Canada.

Certification

Chocolatiers do not require certification, but those who are accredited can expect better employment opportunities and higher wages. Ecole Chocolat offers a certified chocolatier badge that proves that the wearer understands cocoa bean processing practices, the chemistry of chocolate, and advanced chocolate-making skills.

Some states require commercial food makers to take an accredited food safety certification program every five years. The National Restaurant Association offers the industry standard ServSafe training and certification programs including the ServSafe Food Handler certification, which is available to all food service employees.

Skills and Personality

Chocolatiers are artists who use their creativity to design and handcraft confections that are both gorgeous and delicious. They need to draw upon their technical knowledge to understand chocolate and how the scientific properties of cocoa, sugar, milk, and other ingredients can be best blended into edible art. Chocolatiers develop their palates to better discern the mix of flavors in their creations. And they have the physical dexterity necessary to perform delicate work with hot, liquid chocolate and other foods.

When they are not creating chocolates, most chocolatiers spend time researching and experimenting. They might study historical uses of chocolate and traditional recipes and ingredients and then delve into the latest food trends on social media. The goal is to create unique confections.

Good business sense is a plus for those who wish to run their own companies. Chocolatiers need to understand finances, marketing, and employee management.

On the Job

Employers

Chocolatiers have a choice of employment options. Some artisan chocolatiers are self-employed entrepreneurs who run their own businesses alone or with a small staff. A larger percentage of chocolatiers work in upscale restaurants, where they plan dessert menus and oversee the production of chocolate confections on a daily basis.

Around 97 percent of the chocolate trade is controlled by multinational corporations like the Hershey Company—famous for Hershey's Kisses and other products—and the Kraft Heinz Company,

Handmade Chocolate in a Pretty Package

"I currently work from my home kitchen and operate B Cocoa Artisan Chocolate as a mobile chocolate shop with local delivery in my city. . . . I also offer chocolate parties and workshops where I go to people's homes or offices. . . . [I worked] to make B Cocoa Artisan Chocolate appear professional enough that my clients would never guess I did most of my work from home. . . . Your product and your packaging must work together. It can mean the difference between appearing as a hobby chocolatier and selling to your neighbor next door, and appearing professional enough that corporations want to gift your chocolate to their clients."

—Brooke Willis, owner of B Cocoa Artisan Chocolate

Brooke Willis, "Building a Chocolate Brand Part 1: The First Step to Building a Chocolate Brand—Naming Your Chocolate Business," *Chocolate Blog,* Ecole Chocolat. www.ecolechocolat.com.

which makes Cadbury, Ghirardelli, and other well-known brands. Chocolatiers that work for these industrial-scale chocolate companies might formulate new recipes in test kitchens and work with cooks, marketing staff, and others to bring new products to market.

Working Conditions

Chocolatiers work full-time, and they often put in overtime when projects demand it. Like all kitchen work, making chocolates can be stressful. Chocolatiers are often under pressure to produce flawless creations as quickly as possible. And once a project with liquid chocolate is started, the work cannot stop until it is completed. There is always a risk of severe burns when working with piping hot chocolate.

Earnings and Advancement

In 2025 the average annual wage for chocolatiers was $43,981, according to the employment website ZipRecruiter. However, those who worked in the San Francisco Bay area were able to earn nearly $10,000 more annually. While there are no official figures, those who own successful chocolate boutiques or online stores can expect to earn above the national average.

What Is the Future Outlook for Chocolatiers?

Premium chocolates will never go out of style as long as people continue to celebrate birthdays, anniversaries, and Valentine's Day. There is also a growing demand for vegan and other more healthful chocolate offerings. Accordingly, employment for chocolatiers is expected to grow by around 6 percent through 2034, per the business website Future Market Insights.

Find Out More

Ecole Chocolat Professional School of Chocolate Arts
www.ecolechocolat.com
This school of chocolate arts offers professional chocolatier programs online. It provides students with a virtual interactive classroom that includes tutorial videos, podcasts, blogs, and recipes.

Fine Cacao and Chocolate Institute (FCCI)
www.chocolateinstitute.org
The FCCI is an educational organization that promotes ethical and sustainable practices throughout the chocolate business. The website features an education program, research fellowships, and access to publications.

Fine Chocolate Industry Association (FCIA)
www.finechocolateindustry.org
The FCIA is a trade organization dedicated to promoting the art and business of fine chocolates. The association's website features comprehensive information about chocolate and the industry and offers news, webinars, and student membership discounts.

What Does an Executive Chef Do?

In the late 1980s, when William Bradley was fourteen years old, his aunt gave him a thick cooking encyclopedia called *Larousse Gastronomique*, published in Paris in 1938. Most teens would not be thrilled to receive an encyclopedia for a gift, let alone one that was filled with dense text and no pictures. But Bradley was amazed by the hundreds of recipes for French dishes and the alphabetized descriptions of ingredients and cooking techniques. Bradley was already interested in cooking, but the gift helped solidify his goal in life: he wanted to become an executive chef. By the time he was sixteen, Bradley was working in the kitchen of an Italian restaurant in San Diego. In his twenties, he became a sous chef after training with Chef James Boyce at the Azzura Point in Coronado, California. Bradley was around thirty when he opened Addison, a French-inspired fine dining restaurant in Carmel Valley, a San Diego suburb.

Addison instantly became one of the most fashionable dining spots in San Diego. By 2024 the restaurant had earned three stars from the

At a Glance

Number of Jobs
187,100*

Pay
$58,920 in 2023*

Educational Requirements
Associate's degree recommended

Personal Qualities
Hard worker, creative, committed to quality, good communicator, lifelong learner

Working Conditions
Full-time with overtime, nights, weekends, and holidays

Future Job Outlook
Growth of 8 percent through 2033*

* For all chefs and head cooks

prestigious Michelin Guide. In addition to running one of the most highly rated restaurants in the country, Bradley continues to collect vintage cookbooks. "Cookbooks are a light into the soul of a chef," says Bradley. "In my generation, we didn't see all these big figure chefs on TV and everywhere else. Books were really how you got to know their thinking."[19]

Executive chefs like Bradley have more status than head chefs who run most restaurant kitchens. Executive chefs work at the most expensive fine dining restaurants and at posh resort kitchens, casinos, commercial kitchens, or restaurants that have more than one location. While head chefs prepare food and oversee kitchen staff, executive chefs have many more responsibilities. Culinary arts educator Stephanie White explains,

> Executive chefs are at the top of the kitchen hierarchy. They are responsible for making decisions that affect everything that happens in the kitchen, including what's on the menu, where the ingredients are sourced, and how they should be prepared. The nature of these responsibilities means that, even though "chef" is in their job title, they may rarely prepare the food. The traditional role of an executive chef is much more oriented toward management than cooking.[20]

Whether or not they prepare food daily, executive chefs possess all the cooking skills of a head chef. But executive chefs use their knowledge of ingredients, food trends, cooking techniques, and cuisines of many cultures to create exceptional menus. And executive chefs decide how every dish that leaves the kitchen will be plated and presented to diners.

Executive chefs use their managerial skills to monitor food costs when creating menus to ensure that their offerings are profitable. They are involved in creating restaurant budgets, setting staff levels and work protocols, and conducting performance reviews.

Executive chefs are versed in the use of a wide range of kitchen and cooking equipment, including meat slicers, grinders, deep fryers, ranges, ovens, and walk-in coolers, and they arrange the purchase of new equipment when necessary. Executive chefs also make sure the strictest hygiene and food safety standards are followed by kitchen staff.

How Do You Become an Executive Chef?

Education and Training

Some of the world's most famous, award-winning executive chefs—including Jamie Oliver and Gordon Ramsay—are self-taught. Most who never attend culinary school begin their careers during their teens like Bradley as entry-level kitchen staff. They gain experience over many years and work their way up to the executive chef position. However, attaining the prestigious title of executive chef is a goal for many in the culinary industry. The best way to stand out among the competition is to obtain a two-year associate's degree in culinary arts.

Students enrolled in community colleges and culinary institutes gain valuable hands-on experience. They learn about international cuisines, essential cooking techniques, food safety and sanitation methods, food presentation, and menu development.

In 2025 there were more than 330 culinary arts schools in the United States offering associate's degrees. Those who hope to become executive chefs can go on to earn a four-year bachelor's degree in culinary arts. Bachelor's programs focus on advanced skills in cooking, restaurant finance and marketing, sustainable business practices, and restaurant research and development.

Internships and Mentorships

Culinary school graduates will find it easier to launch their careers if they work as interns or with mentors. While mentorship programs have a slight overlap with internships, interns generally

The Importance of Mentorships

"The restaurant industry, a fast-paced dominion that demands continual change, thrives off of creativity, innovation, and the mastery of the culinary arts. Amid the hustle and bustle, a secret force propels future culinary stars' growth and development to be extraordinary within the culinary arts: mentors. Mentorship, in the world of chefs, is a sacred alliance that transcends the boundaries of a kitchen. It is the bridge that connects tradition with innovation, technique with creativity, and novice with maestro. Just as a chef imparts flavors into a dish, mentors infuse knowledge, skills, and guidance into the aspiring minds of future chefs."

—Peter McQuaid, executive chef

Quoted in Joyce Appleman, "Nurturing Excellence: The Crucial Role of Mentorship in the Dynamic Restaurant Industry," Total Food Service, September 21, 2023. https://totalfood.com.

have more developed skills. Most culinary academies host internship and mentorship programs that pair students with restaurants and executive chefs. The American Culinary Federation selects mentorship participants through an online application process.

Many of the world's greatest chefs learned discipline, leadership, teamwork, cooking, and business skills while working with one or more mentors. Most feel that their mentorship was a life-changing experience. Executive chef Tae Strain says his mentorship with executive chef Stuart Brioza helped him in the early days of his career. Strain insists, "No one has taught me more about food, ingredients, and culture than him. His energy was unlike anyone else I had been around, and there was a constant pursuit and cultivation of intangible qualities in the food and restaurant at large."[21]

Certification and Licensing

Culinary schools and other restaurant institutes offer certification for executive chefs. Those who are accredited have better

Executive chef William Bradley prepares baby cauliflower in the Addison kitchen during the restaurant's early years. Executive chefs decide what will be on the menu, where to source ingredients, and how they should be prepared.

job prospects and earning opportunities in the highly competitive restaurant industry. The most widely recognized certifications are issued by the American Culinary Federation, which offers more than a dozen levels of industry-recognized accreditation. Those seeking the highest-level designation, certified executive chef, are required to have at least an associate's degree in culinary arts, five years of job experience, and supervisory experience with at least five full-time workers. Certification is awarded after completion of six thirty-hour courses that focus on nutrition, food safety, management, cost control, and other topics. Applicants are required to pass one written exam and one practical exam that demonstrate their abilities.

Skills and Personality

Executive chefs are creative food artists who improve old recipes, develop new ones, and find unique ways to present dishes with a flair. Beyond food artistry, chefs need a good business sense to efficiently produce meals that are profitable for their restaurant. Serving fresh, perfectly made dishes for hundreds of customers a day also requires a commitment to quality. As White writes, "Executive chefs must have the attention to detail to make sure each dish gets just the right finish of balsamic glaze or grated truffle, along with the foresight and management skills to train their staff effectively."[22]

As team supervisors, executive chefs need good communication skills. They need to clearly instruct kitchen staff, educate interns, work out the best deals with vendors, and succinctly explain business matters to investors, partners, and others. As Bradley says, "A great chef is not only a great cook but is also a great listener, speaker and someone that has the ability to nurture young professionals."[23]

Executive chefs need to be lifelong learners. Restaurant owner Lance McWhorter recalls, "When I was the executive chef, I still needed to learn. I still needed to grow. Everything about you—your cooking chops, your palate, your knowledge base, your creativity—need to always be expanding."[24]

On the Job

Employers

Executive chefs can find a vast array of employment opportunities at resorts, restaurants, and casinos. Some work as private chefs, however, cooking for wealthy clients or people who have serious illnesses or dietary restrictions. Executive chef Chris Smith was diagnosed with type 2 diabetes while training at the Culinary Institute of America and went on to make a career as "the Diabetic Chef." He teaches cooking classes that focus on eating healthfully and has written several cookbooks.

Working Conditions

Executive chefs work in a fast-paced environment, often more than forty hours a week, including early mornings, late evenings, weekends, and holidays. Maintaining consistent, high-quality

Love the Work and Do Not Give Up

"The first bit of advice I would give someone wanting to go into the culinary world is love what you do. No matter if it's slinging burgers or grilling dry aged steak, you have to love it. If you have that love, then it stops feeling like work and more like fun. You must love the chaos of it as well as the organization. The next bit is don't give up. You can't quit if you ruined a sauce or burnt a steak. You must take those as learning moments and improve. Everyone is going to fail but it's how we get up that makes the difference."

—Mikey T, executive chef

Quoted in Irene San Segundo, "Why This Executive Chef Says Culinary Career Opportunity at Marriott Is 'Unparalleled,'" *The Life at Marriott Blog*, August 20, 2024. https://life.marriott.com.

output from kitchen staff can be stressful, and there are risks of burns, cuts, falls, and other injuries.

Earnings and Advancement

Executive chefs are among the highest-paid professionals in the culinary world, but their salaries vary depending on experience, where they live, and whether they are restaurant owners or employees. According to the BLS, chefs and head cooks of all types were paid a mean annual salary of $58,920 in 2023. However, the BLS says the highest 10 percent of earners, which would include executive chefs, made $93,900 annually. Those like Bradley, who own successful restaurants, earn substantially more. And executive chefs like Guy Fieri, who go on to become TV stars and best-selling authors, can earn tens of millions of dollars.

What Is the Future Outlook for Executive Chefs?

More Americans are eating out every year, and there is a growing demand for high-quality dining experiences. The BLS predicts 8 percent growth through 2033 for all chefs and head cooks. Because of limited opportunities and competition to earn the title of executive chef, though, the growth rate for these positions is likely to be slower.

Find Out More

Culinary Careers Program (C-Cap)
https://culinarycareers.org
C-Cap is a nonprofit workforce development organization dedicated to training the next generation of food and hospitality workers. Programs aimed at high school students provide training in culinary skills and career development. C-Cap also offers scholarships, apprenticeships, and internship opportunities.

Research Chefs Association (RCA)
www.culinology.org
The RCA is dedicated to blending the culinary arts with food science to provide technical information to the food industry. The association offers certification to culinary researchers and provides programs and scholarships to students interested in learning advanced food preparation, safety, and production techniques.

World Association of Chef Societies
www.worldchefs.org
This organization, headquartered in France, works to maintain and improve culinary standards on a global scale. The association provides information about qualified culinary schools, standards for quality culinary education, certification, competitions, and job opportunities.

What Does a Food Stylist Do?

Judging by hundreds of millions of food photos on social media, people love to take pictures of their meals. The photos show everything from half-eaten burgers to decorative dishes. While most of these photos are uploaded by amateurs, some people make a living preparing photogenic food. These professionals, called food stylists, use their creative skills to artfully arrange food items for ads, websites, magazine articles, food blogs and vlogs, and TV programs and movies.

At a Glance

Number of Jobs
64,590 in 2025

Pay
$57,240 in 2025

Educational Requirements
Associate's degree recommended

Personal Qualities
Cooking skills, knowledge of food science, patience, organization, team player

Working Conditions
Full- or part-time, with long hours working in studios preparing and styling food

Future Job Outlook
Growth of 14 percent through 2028

Food stylists work with professional photographers and videographers to present food so that it looks good on camera. They use their artistic skills and extensive knowledge of food to create visually appealing images. Commercial food photographer Christina Peters asserts, "Beautifully plating a dish is one thing, that's hard enough, but knowing how to take difficult foods, ugly foods, foods that don't look so good cooked, or raw, AND THEN plating them beautifully is very difficult."[25]

Food styling should really be called food manipulation, according to Peters. That is because making food items photogenic is more like building a sculpture rather than cooking a recipe. And there are several tricks that stylists use to create seemingly beautiful dishes out of ingredients that are inedible. For example, if a job calls for a photo of a tasty-looking cappuccino, a food stylist might use soap bubbles to give the drink a creamy foam head. Hamburgers are some of the most popular items in ads, but preparing them to be photographed requires a great deal of creativity from the food stylist. The precooked burger is cold and the crosshatch grill marks on top are usually made with carefully applied lighter fluid set aflame. Sesame seeds on top of buns are often applied with tweezers and glue. A delicious-looking stack of pancakes may be propped up with cardboard hidden between the layers. A picture of a perfectly prepared Thanksgiving turkey is likely taken with raw meat sprayed with gravy, water, and food coloring. A blowtorch is used to create a shiny cooked appearance. Ice cream, which quickly melts under hot studio lights, might be colored lard mixed with powdered sugar. And ice cream sundaes are usually whipped up from mashed potatoes covered in chocolate syrup.

Foods stylists work with props such as silverware, plates, tablecloths, and centerpieces. They all possess a food stylist kit filled with tools and substances used to manipulate food. The kit includes scissors, spoons, tweezers, spatulas, and sharp knives. Spray bottles are used to apply droplets of water to foods like strawberries and salads, which look better when glistening. Mustard, ketchup, and other viscous liquids are carefully applied with syringes. Makeup wands and cotton swabs are needed to clean up smudges on foods and remove lint from surfaces. A sticky substance called museum putty, which is sold to hold pictures on a wall, can be employed to hold stacks of brownies or cookies together. Small paintbrushes and paints are used by food stylists to give food eye-popping colors. Toothpicks and T-shaped pins are used to hold sandwiches together. Food photographer

Must Taste Good for TV

"In most cases you're responsible for everything: shopping for the ingredients, cooking the ingredients, [and plating the dish]. You have to know how long the food is going to be on set. How many multiples do you have to make? Is anyone going to eat it? That's a huge deal. . . . If someone's going to take a bite out of a burger, you don't want them to bite into a big toothpick. . . . There's nothing worse than [a TV host] getting a bite of something cold or something gross. That reaction can't be taken away when you're on live TV."

—Lisa Spychala, food stylist

Quoted in Auguste Escoffier School of Culinary Arts, "Pro Food Stylist Lisa Spychala Learns New Tricks at Escoffier," *Success Stories* (blog), February 16, 2023. www.escoffier.edu.

and stylist Regan Baroni explains the importance of a heat gun, which produces extreme, concentrated heat: "It comes in handy for foods like cheeseburgers or pizzas or any food that needs to look 'freshly heated' or melty. A lot of foods are time sensitive and lose that appetite appeal pretty quickly. . . . A heat gun can help you re-capture the perfect melting point even after the food has been sitting for a little while."[26]

Food stylists usually specialize in one of two fields. Editorial food stylists focus on producing photos for magazine articles and cookbooks. Editorial stylists usually cook the dishes and then manipulate the food to look its best on camera. Peters says she has worked on editorial shoots that required her to photograph ten different recipes in a single day. "That might involve additional ingredient shots too," she explains. "That's a ton of food to style in one day in which we are following recipes that we discover sometimes . . . were not tested all that well. Now, the food stylist has to get really creative to fix some recipes, and make the food look nice. Very challenging on a low budget."[27]

Advertising food stylists, as the name implies, work on photo shoots for ads seen in magazines, e-commerce sites, social media campaigns, and catalogs as well as on food packages, billboards, and restaurant websites and menus. Those who work on TV and movie sets are often required to use real foods—actors do not want to eat ice cream made from lard. Food stylists for films need to have a different approach, according to Chris Oliver, who has styled foods for numerous TV shows. "Realistic food is not all beautiful and perfect. I make ugly food and burnt food, too,"[28] he says.

How Do You Become a Food Stylist?

Education and Training

Most food stylists have a degree in culinary arts, and many have previously worked as chefs in restaurants or commercial kitchens. Elle Simone Scott, the food stylist on the TV show *America's Test Kitchen,* encourages others to train at a culinary institute. She says, "I like to remind people that all food stylists are chefs, but not all chefs are food stylists."[29] Hollywood food stylist Brett Long insists he was inspired to pursue his career after he saw a food fight in the 1991 movie *Hook.* "Everything is super brightly colored, nice amorphous shapes and blobby texture," he recalls. "I'd never been so jealous of being in a food fight in my entire life."[30] Long went on to attend a culinary institute where he studied to become a pastry chef.

Peters says that after obtaining an education in the culinary arts, graduates should try to find work as assistants to professional food stylists: "You [need] training to do this. This means assisting other food stylists who do this full time, for a living. It takes several years working with a food styling team before you branch out and call yourself a food stylist on your own."[31]

Internships

After earning an associate's degree, Long worked as an intern at a cookbook publishing company. He watched food stylists as they created photos for cookbooks and drew on his pastry chef experience to help arrange food at photo shoots. This allowed him to build a portfolio of work that he used when he moved on to food styling full-time.

Certification and Licensing

There are no specific certifications for food stylists. However, those who attain accreditation as a certified baker, certified decorator, certified executive pastry chef, or certified master chef can expect better work opportunities. Additionally, a food handler's license is necessary for those who prepare edible foods that are consumed by actors on-screen.

Skills and Personality

Food stylists need a good understanding of food science. Some foods last three hours under studio lights, whereas others can only be used for three minutes. Stylists need to know how foods behave and when substitutions might be necessary.

Food stylists are team players; they work with camera teams, lighting techs, food vendors, advertising executives, and others. Good time-management and organizational skills are a must. Food stylists must arrive at a photo shoot with all the ingredients and equipment they might need. This includes enough food to last through fifteen or twenty takes at a session that might last twelve hours or more. And setting and resetting shots requires extreme patience and the ability to work in tiring and stressful situations.

On the Job

Employers

Most food stylists are self-employed. Freelancers take gigs with food bloggers and websites, meal delivery services, and independent restaurants. Some who work full-time are employed by food manufacturers, restaurant chains, cookbook publishers, magazines, and ad agencies.

A food stylist prepares a strawberry-topped slice of cheesecake for a photo shoot. Food stylists use all sorts of techniques and ingredients to make food look visually appealing online and in print.

Working Conditions

Food stylists work long days under hot lights. The job requires travel to grocery stores, kitchen suppliers, and photo and video shoot sets. The work is fast paced and can be extremely demanding. Unpredictable conditions are the rule because foods often wilt, spoil, melt, fall apart, and otherwise become unusable. Food stylists who cannot meet the high expectations of their clients can find themselves without work.

Earnings and Advancement

The employment website Glassdoor says that food stylists earned an average annual income of $57,240 in 2025. But those who work on TV commercials, TV shows, and movies can earn more. Hollywood food stylists who belong to the International Alliance of Theatrical Stage Employees union are guaranteed an hourly rate of $45 to $65 an hour. And Long says he earns a considerably higher wage: "If you're being brought in for a commercial

Learn to Cook First

"It's pretty vital to have a cooking qualification from a reputed cooking school. . . . If you assist someone they want to know you can chop, cook and move fast. There are lots of stylists, like me, who are self-taught, but nowadays that's rare. Working as a food stylist you have to know how to cook everything from pastry and a three-layer cake to a joint of meat. There isn't time on a job to start looking things up—you need extensive knowledge about all types of food."

—Jennifer Joyce, food stylist

Jennifer Joyce, "How to Become a Food Stylist: Jennifer Joyce," Good Food, 2025. www.bbcgoodfood.com.

that's food-heavy, and you're the lead stylist, and you're working for up to a week, [the rate might be $1,250 a day]."[32] By Long's calculation a stylist would only need to work around forty-six days in a year to earn the Glassdoor average. And most who have experience and good contacts in the business generally work more often.

What Is the Future Outlook for Food Stylists?

Photos and videos of beautifully styled food are in demand everywhere from social media and online magazines to TV commercials and billboards. With food marketing playing an increasingly important role, the demand for food stylists is expected to grow by 14 percent through 2028, according to the career website Zippia.

Find Out More

American Society of Media Photographers (ASMP)

www.asmp.org

The ASMP provides news articles and videos related to media photography that can be helpful for food stylists. The society's website provides a platform for photographers to showcase their work and helps members connect with new clients. It also holds a program for students.

International Association of Culinary Professionals (IACP)

www.iacpculinary.com

The IACP offers education and mentorship to culinary professionals. The website features blogs, employment opportunities, résumé-writing services, and career advice.

National Restaurant Association

www.restaurant.org

The National Restaurant Association is an education, certification, and job-development organization for the restaurant industry. The association offers information about scholarships, food trends, tech innovations, and menu development.

What Does a Craft Brewer Do?

In 1797 a ship called the *Sydney Cove* sank in the treacherous waters off the coast of southern Australia. Several dozen bottles of beer went beneath the waves along with the rest of the cargo. The beer survived for more than two centuries in the icy ocean waters until the bottles were brought to the surface by divers on a salvage expedition. In 2018 craft brewers working at the James Squire craft brewery in Sydney were able to use the still-active yeast in the ancient beer to brew up new batches of dark porter-style beer called "The Wreck Preservation Ale." Haydon Morgan, the head brewer on the project, said at the time, "This particular yeast was very temperamental and had a thirst for life, so it took a lot of trial and error to find the right balance. After a lot of different recipes, we decided it was perfect for a porter style."[33]

Craft brewers like Morgan are sometimes called brewmasters or head brewers. They oversee every step of making beer, which is one of the oldest recorded crafts. Every year large multinational brewers such as Anheuser-Busch InBev

At a Glance

Number of Jobs
49,740 in 2023

Pay
$56,040 in 2025

Educational Requirements
Certificate from brewery institute recommended

Personal Qualities
Creative, scientifically and mechanically inclined, physically fit, cooking skills

Working Conditions
Brewers work long days in hot breweries scrubbing, bending, climbing, standing, and lifting

Future Job Outlook
Growth of 4 percent through 2030

and Molson Coors produce around three-quarters of all beer sold in the United States. But according to the data website Statista there were more than 9,760 US craft breweries in 2023, an all-time high. Craft breweries are smaller, independent companies that make handcrafted beer using traditional brewing methods. In 2023 craft breweries sold nearly $29 billion worth of beer, according to the craft beer trade group Brewers Association. Food writer Mallika Khandelwal says that craft breweries are thriving because consumers "are bored with the limited options that the big brewing companies offer and want more choosing power. Craft breweries continually launch new beers and limited runs of unique beers, so customers always have options for different sampling flavors."[34]

Around 99 percent of all American breweries are craft breweries, which can be classified as either brewpubs or microbreweries. Brewpubs are restaurant that serve food and make beer on the premises. Microbreweries are small beer factories where beer is brewed and put in bottles, cans, or kegs for sale in taverns, liquor retailers, supermarkets, and other stores.

Most craft beer is made from water, yeast, barley, and hops—the flowers of the hop plant. Craft brewers oversee the scientific process that turns the starch in barley into a type of sugar called malt. The malt feeds yeast, which converts the sugar into alcohol and carbon dioxide, or beer bubbles. Hops work as a preservative and flavoring agent that provides beer with a desirable bitterness that balances out the sweetness of the malt. Basic beer ingredients are used to make dozens of different styles with names like pilsner, porter, stout, bock, and pale ale. In addition to understanding traditional recipes, craft brewers invent their own versions of each style to differentiate their beers from hundreds of others brewed by competitors. They do this by changing recipes or reinventing them by adding wheat, rye, fruits, spices, or special ingredients that might include coffee, maple syrup, or even cherries and raspberries.

While craft brewers rely on artistic flair to create new recipes, the brewing process involves controlling a massive copper and stainless steel brewing system. On a typical brewing day, a craft brewer will grind hundreds of pounds of barley grain. This is added to water in a giant gas-fired cooking vessel called a mash tun. The barley, which looks like a giant bowl of oatmeal, is held at various temperatures to create a sweet juice called mash. The mash is fed into a giant strainer called a lauter tun that separates the liquid from the spent grain. The liquid, called wort, is transferred to a brew kettle where it is boiled for an hour or more. The craft brewer adds hops at various stages of the process. The wort is cooled down, the brewer adds the yeast, and the liquid ferments over the course of several weeks. The fermented beer is then moved to conditioning tanks to clarify and age for a month or more.

Warm wort and yeast attract all sorts of invisible bacteria that can adversely affect the taste, smell, and quality of beer. When a batch of bad beer goes down the drain, it can cost the brewery thousands of dollars. For that reason, craft brewers spend most of their days cleaning and sanitizing brewing equipment with harsh chemicals while dressed in rubber boots, gloves, aprons, and goggles. Jon Lang, head brewer at the Triton Brewing Company in Indianapolis, says that for every hour spent brewing, he spends three hours cleaning: “We’re janitors first, and brewers second. . . . [Cleaning is] mostly what we do, with sporadic bursts of brewing in between.”[35]

Specialists known as technical brewers do not run large brewing systems. They experiment with various ingredients and make beer in small batches. The goal is to create recipes that can be scaled up and introduced to the public as new brews. Australian technical brewer Glenn Harrison explains, “Every time a new ingredient comes out I can do a hundred experiments with it. I’m learning stuff all the time.”[36]

The Role of a Technical Brewer

"A large part of this [job] is experimenting with ingredients on our pilot brewery so we can really understand how they work in various conditions. We then pass that information on to brewers before they start using them to make sure they get the most out of them. I also offer brewers practical help on brewing issues they may have, advice on process improvement, and occasionally assist with recipe development too. . . . The other part of my role is more about education and imparting my knowledge and experience to less experienced brewers in the industry."

—Glenn Harrison, technical brewer

Quoted in James Smith, "A Day in the Life Of: A Technical Brewer," The Crafty Pint, April 7, 2021. https://craftypint.com.

All craft brewers in the United States deal with paperwork and bureaucracy. Brewing is regulated and taxed at the federal level by the Bureau of Alcohol, Tobacco, Firearms, and Explosives. Beer is measured in a unit called a barrel, which is equal to 31 gallons (159 L). Craft brewers are required to fill out reports every two weeks that provide details about the exact number of barrels they brewed and the exact amount of beer that was spilled or wasted during operations. Additional paperwork is required by individual states, which also tax beer production.

How Do You Become a Craft Brewer?

Education and Training

It is against the law for anyone under the age of twenty-one to make or consume beer or other alcoholic beverages, so most craft brewers do not learn their trade in high school or even at undergrad courses in college. Many do, however, begin their careers as homebrewers who make beer in their kitchens. But with the continued growth of the craft beer industry, owners and managers

A craft brewer prepares to sample his work. Craft brewers rely on artistic flair to create new recipes. However, the brewing process is highly controlled within large copper and stainless-steel tanks.

of craft breweries are less inclined to hire untrained brewing staff. Most prefer employees who have a good understanding of brewing science and operations. Prospective brewers can take courses through the educational program known as the World Brewing Academy (WBA), which is offered by the Siebel Institute of Technology in Chicago. The WBA course catalog includes the Concise Course in Brewing Technology, the Advanced Brewing Theory program, and the Master Brewer program. There are also numerous university-affiliated programs offered at institutions throughout the United States and Canada.

Internships

Prospective brewers often start their careers as volunteers or interns. Craft brewers jokingly call this type of labor "working in the rat cellar," which refers to previous centuries when barrels and brewing supplies were kept in a brewery's basement. These "cellar rats" perform a lot of cleaning and sanitation duties. Interns are also expected to off-load sacks of grain from trucks, work on bottling lines, and perform other tough physical jobs.

Certification and Licensing

As with most professions, certification helps craft brewers enhance their job prospects and earn higher salaries. The University of California, Davis, extension program offers a fifteen-week Master Brewers Certificate Program that can be taken in person or online. The certificate shows that the holder is held to the highest brewing industry standards.

Skills and Personality

Successful craft brewers combine creativity, scientific knowledge, and hard physical work. They are passionate about beer and brewing, attuned to the subtle flavor profiles of various brews, and knowledgeable about the methods and processes used to create each style. Brewers must know how to use scientific instruments to measure bitterness, yeast viability, color, and other factors. They need to be mechanically inclined to operate industrial brewing equipment and in good physical shape to engage in the hard work of making beer.

On the Job

Employers

Most craft brewers work at microbreweries and brewpubs. Some can also be found working at regional breweries with annual beer production of between 15,000 and 6 million barrels. Regional breweries tend be older facilities like the Jacob Leinenkugel Brewing Company in Chippewa Falls, Wisconsin.

Working Conditions

From start to finish, the brewing process takes eight to twelve hours. Brewers are on their feet most of the time, working in conditions

A Woman Making a Difference

"I quickly made a plan to get into a [beer brewing] program. . . . At this point I drank beer, but only really light beers or sours. I mostly liked the culture and community within the industry. The idea that [a woman] could create beverages and a space that would bring people together was my driving force to this career path, fueled by the idea that by just entering into this space I could be creating change. . . . Brewing was and is still a primarily male oriented industry and I could be a small part of the work being done to make a difference."

—Ceridwyn Thibert, student craft brewer

Ceridwyn Thibert, "The Life of a Future Brewer," *The Growler,* June 21, 2024. https://on.thegrowler.ca.

that are often hot, humid, and slippery. Brewers clean with harsh chemicals, climb on platforms, scale ladders connected to brewing equipment, and regularly lift 50 pound (23 kg) sacks of grain. Brewers also tend to drink a lot of beer, which is associated with certain health problems.

Earnings and Advancement

In 2023 the Brewers Association released a detailed salary report that covered dozens of jobs in the craft brewing industry. The report says that craft brewers earned an average annual salary of $56,040. Those employed as head brewers or assistant brewmasters brought in $72,556. Brewmasters with ten or more years of experience could expect to earn $112,481.

What Is the Future Outlook for Craft Brewers?

The craft brewing market is facing challenges. Labor and ingredient costs are rising, and health-conscious consumers are drinking less beer. However, according to the Brewers Association, the craft beer industry supported nearly 460,000 jobs nationwide in 2024, and demand for craft brewers is expected to grow by 4 percent through 2030.

Find Out More

American Brewers Guild (ABG)

www.abgbrew.com

The ABG is a brewing school that offers online and on-site classroom instruction, including two comprehensive brewing diploma programs: the Intensive Brewing Science and Engineering Program and the Craftbrewer's Apprenticeship Program. The guild offers employment services and other career development information.

American Society of Brewing Chemists (ASBC)

www.asbcnet.org

The ASBC is a scientific organization that represents large and small breweries. The society's website provides scholarship information and career advice for brewers and brewing specialists.

Brewers Association (BA)

www.brewersassociation.org

The BA is a trade organization that represents the craft beer industry. The BA website provides numerous resources for prospective brewers with links to industry statistics, career resources, brewing publications, and brewing schools and organizations.

Source Notes

Introduction: The Art of Cooking

1. Quoted in Kirk Bachmann, "How to Create Unforgettable Food Memories: Executive Chef Lee Hillson," *The Ultimate Dish* (podcast), episode 59, September 13, 2022. www.escoffier.edu.
2. Quoted in Bachmann, "How to Create Unforgettable Food Memories."
3. Bentley, "What Can a Prep/Line Cook Do to Move Up to Manager?," Quora, 2023. www.quora.com.
4. James Constantine Frangos, "James Constantine's Answer," reply to "What [Are] All the Culinary Paths?," CareerVillage.org, November 17, 2023. www.careervillage.org.

Pastry Chef

5. Quoted in Josué A. Cruz, "Why Save Room for Dessert," *Edible Northeast Florida,* May 27, 2019. https://ediblenortheastflorida.ediblecommunities.com.
6. Quoted in AnnMarie Mattila, "Pierre Hermé: The 'King of Modern Patisserie,'" *Pastry Arts Magazine,* December 2, 2020. https://pastryartsmag.com.
7. Precious Pioneer, "What Is It Like Working as a Pastry Chef?," Medium, February 27, 2023. https://preciouspioneer.medium.com.
8. Quoted in Auguste Escoffier School of Culinary Arts, "Master Baker Colette Christian on Perseverance and Never Giving Up," *Baking and Pastry Arts* (blog), March 19, 2021. www.escoffier.edu.
9. Quoted in Wild Leaven Bakery, "Internship Success Story: Katie Medina," August 30, 2023. https://wildleavenbakery.com.

Sushi Chef

10. Warren Ransom, "A Day in the Life of a Sushi Chef," SushiFAQ.com, June 26, 2024. www.sushifaq.com.

11. Kevin Kilcoyne, "Becoming a Sushi Chef: Mastering the Craft," Kokoro Care, September 28, 2021. https://kokorocares.com.
12. Quoted in Alvin Lim, "The Importance of Shari in Sushi, According to a Michelin Starred Chef," Michelin Guide, October 3, 2024. https://guide.michelin.com.
13. Ransom, "A Day in the Life of a Sushi Chef."
14. Quoted in Mischa van den Burg, "I'm in Love with My Work: Lessons from a Japanese Sushi Master," *Mischa van den Burg* (blog), October 8, 2022. https://mischavandenburg.com.

Chocolatier

15. Quoted in Kirk Bachmann, "How Chocolatier Katrina Markoff Created a Celebrated Luxury Chocolate Brand," *The Ultimate Dish* (podcast), episode 32, March 1, 2022. www.escoffier.edu.
16. Estelle Tracy, "I'm in the Joy Business," 37 Chocolates, October 4, 2023. https://37chocolates.com.
17. Mark Schimmel, "Bean-to-Bar Chocolate: What Is It and Why It Matters," Krak Chocolade, July 12, 2023. https://medium.com.
18. Quoted in Purdys Chocolatier, "Becoming a Chocolatier: Spilling the Beans on This Tasty Career Choice," *Purdys Blog,* June 1, 2018. www.purdys.com.

Executive Chef

19. Quoted in Marguerite Imbert, "Inside William Bradley's Cookbook Collection," Michelin Guide, October 8, 2019. https://guide.michelin.com.
20. Stephanie White, "Executive Chef vs Head Chef: What Is the Difference?," *Culinary & Pastry Careers* (blog), Auguste Escoffier School of Culinary Arts, July 3, 2024. www.escoffier.edu.
21. Quoted in Morgan Goldberg, "How I Got My Job: Running My Own Pop-Up After Years as an Executive Chef in D.C.," Eater, February 10, 2023. www.eater.com.
22. White, "Executive Chef vs Head Chef."
23. Quoted in Ment'or, "Chef Spotlight: William Bradley," 2025. www.mentorbkb.org.
24. Quoted in White, "Executive Chef vs Head Chef."

Food Stylist

25. Christina Peters, "What Is a Food Stylist and What You Need to Know If You Are Calling Yourself One," *Food Photography Blog*. https://foodphotographyblog.com.
26. Regan Baroni, "The Best Food Styling Tools for Food Photography," *Regan Baroni* (blog). https://reganbaroni.com.
27. Peters, "What Is a Food Stylist and What You Need to Know If You Are Calling Yourself One."
28. Quoted in Alyson Sheppard, "14 Behind-the-Scenes Secrets of Hollywood Food Stylists," Mental Floss, February 16, 2018. www.mentalfloss.com.
29. Quoted in Jillian Kramer, "How to Become a Food Stylist," *Food & Wine*, September 15, 2022. www.foodandwine.com.
30. Quoted in Betty Hallock, "Explaining Hollywood: How to Get a Job as a Food Stylist," *Los Angeles Times,* January 11, 2023. www.latimes.com.
31. Peters, "What Is a Food Stylist and What You Need to Know If You Are Calling Yourself One."
32. Quoted in Hallock, "Explaining Hollywood."

Craft Brewer

33. Quoted in Maris Fessenden, "Australian Brewers Are Making Beer from Yeast Found on a Shipwreck," *Smithsonian,* May 7, 2018. www.smithsonianmag.com.
34. Mallika Khandelwal, "5 Reasons Small Breweries and Craft Beer Companies Are Thriving," *OpenGrowth* (blog), December 16, 2022. www.blogs.opengrowth.com.
35. Quoted in Justin Knepp, "It's More Than Just the Beer: A Day in the Life of an Indiana Craft Brewery," Indiana On Tap, May 27, 2024. https://indianaontap.com.
36. Quoted in James Smith, "A Day in the Life Of: A Technical Brewer," The Crafty Pint, April 7, 2021. https://craftypint.com.

Interview with a Sushi Chef

Soichi Kadoya has worked as a sushi chef for more than twenty-five years. He is currently the head sushi chef and owner of Soichi Sushi, a Michelin-starred restaurant in San Diego, California. He answered these questions during an in-person interview. Comments have been edited for length and clarity.

Q: Why did you become a sushi chef?

A: When I was a little kid in Tokyo, I never thought I wanted to be a sushi chef, but I liked cooking. Both my parents were working, so I started cooking ramen noodles and other foods to feed myself. Also, my dad loved cooking fish. He would go fishing and bring the catch back home. He taught me how to cook fish, and I liked that. I worked as an apprentice sushi chef for around five years in Tokyo and worked in other kinds of restaurants. When I moved to San Diego in 1999, my experience helped me find work as a sushi chef right away.

Q: Can you describe your typical workday?

A: Any chef job means working long, long hours. I own a restaurant, so I wake up and check the day's reservations online and in emails. Around 10:00 a.m. I go shopping for some of the ingredients I need. I get my fish from a vendor in Tokyo, and I make calls and write emails to make sure I will get the [best] tuna, salmon, yellowtail, and other high-grade fish. I start cutting fish around 12:00 p.m. I slice off the skin and fillet the fish into strips and cubes. Around 3:30 or 4:00, I take a thirty-minute break. I open up the restaurant at 4:30 p.m. and prepare sushi and interact with customers until they are all gone, around 11:00 at night. Then I spend an hour or so cleaning up and dealing with paperwork and other tasks.

Q: What do you like most about your job?
A: I like everything, but what I like most is serving the customers up front at the sushi bar. I can communicate with the customers and see their reaction when they eat the sushi I prepare. And we have fun together. The sushi bar is my thing, and some customers treat me like a rock star.

Q: What do you like least about your job?
A: All day I'm standing up. I don't sit for more than thirty minutes in a single day. It's pretty hard, and sometimes my body is kind of screaming.

Q: What personal qualities do you find most valuable for this type of work?
A: You have to love to cook and interact with customers. If you were super shy and working in front of customers, that would be pretty tough. You have to have discipline to be able to continually perform the many small tasks that are part of your daily routine.

Q: What can you share with students about hocho (sushi knives)?
A: Every sushi chef has his own knives from Japan, specially designed for sushi. Some can cost a couple thousand dollars for one knife. That's kind of fancy though; I don't use those. You have to keep the knives razor sharp, sharpening them sometimes twice a day because we need a good clean cut. It makes all the difference in the taste of the sushi and how it looks. We use a whetstone, also from Japan. I still have all my fingers, but I get cut a lot. And it takes a long time to heal.

Q: What advice do you have for students who might be interested in this career?
A: You have to love to serve customers and love cooking. You need love to create. With sushi, each piece needs to be special, so it's not just doing the exact same thing over and over. And each customer is different. You have to understand their tastes. And you have to love fish.

Other Jobs in the Culinary Arts

- Bakery worker
- Barista
- Bartender
- Beekeeper
- Bottling line supervisor
- Brewery laborer
- Butcher
- Cake decorator
- Catering manager
- Cheese maker
- Cook
- Food buyer
- Food preparation worker
- Food product taster
- Food safety specialist
- Food service manager
- Food technologist
- Fry cook
- Grocery store consultant
- Institutional chef
- Kitchen facilities designer
- Line cook
- Mixologist
- Nutritionist
- Restaurant manager
- School food service director
- Server
- Sous chef
- Sustainability specialist
- Wine steward
- Winemaker

Editor's note: The online *Occupational Outlook Handbook* of the US Department of Labor's Bureau of Labor Statistics is an excellent source of information on jobs in hundreds of career fields, including many of those listed here. The *Occupational Outlook Handbook* may be accessed online at www.bls.gov/ooh.

Index

Note: Boldface page numbers indicate illustrations.

advertising food stylists, 41
American Brewers Guild (ABG), 53
American Culinary Federation (ACF), 10, 13, 33, 34
American Society of Brewing Chemists (ASBC), 53
American Society of Media Photographers (ASMP), 44–45
America's Test Kitchen (TV program), 41
Association for the Advancement of the Japanese Culinary Arts (AAJ), 21

bakery clubs, 9
Baroni, Regan, 39–40
bean-to-bar chocolate, 24
beer/beer brewing
  ingredients in, 47
  process of, 48
  regulation of, 49
Bentley (online chef), 5
Boyce, James, 30
Bradley, William, 30–31, **34**, 35, 36
Bragard, Benjamin, 20
Brewers Association (BA), 52–53, 53
brewpubs, 47
Brioza, Stuart, 33
Bureau of Alcohol, Tobacco, and Firearms, 49
Bureau of Labor Statistics (BLS), 5
  on executive chef, 36–37
  on jobs in culinary arts, 5, 59
  on pastry chef, 12, 13

cake designers, 7
chocolatier, **26**
  certification, 25–26
  education/training requirements for, 22, 24–25
  employers of, 27–28
  future job outlook for, 22, 29
  information on, 29
  internships, 25
  number of jobs for, 22
  role of, 22–24
  salary/earnings for, 22, 28–29
  skills/personal qualities of, 22, 27
  working conditions for, 22, 28
Christianson, Collette, 8
cocoa beans, 23
confectioners, 7
craft brewer, **50**
  certification/licensing, 51
  education/training requirements for, 46, 49–50
  employers of, 51

future job outlook for, 46, 52–53
information on, 53
internships, 50–51
number of jobs for, 46
role of, 46–49
salary/earnings for, 46, 52
skills/personal qualities of, 46, 51
working conditions for, 46, 51–52
culinary arts
degrees in, 5
other jobs in, 59
Culinary Careers Program (C-Cap), 37
Culinary Institute of America, 9

deshi (apprentice sushi chef), 16–17

Ecole Chocolat Professional School of Chocolate Arts, 23, 29
editorial food stylists, 40
executive chef, **34**
certification/licensing, 33–34
education/training requirements for, 30, 32
employers of, 35
future job outlook for, 30, 36–37
information on, 37
internships/mentorships, 32–33
number of jobs for, 30
role of, 30–32
salary/earnings for, 30, 36
skills/personal qualities of, 30, 34–35
working conditions for, 30, 35–36

Fieri, Guy, 36
Fine Chocolate Industry Association (FCIA), 29
flavonoids, 23
food stylist, **43**
certification/licensing, 42
education/training requirements for, 38, 41
employers of, 42
future job outlook for, 38, 44
information on, 44–45
internships, 41–42
number of jobs for, 38
role of, 38–41
salary/earnings for, 38, 43–44
skills/personal qualities of, 38, 42
working conditions for, 38, 4 3
Frangos, James Constantine, 5
frozen dessert specialists, 7
Fuji Food Products (FFP), 19, 20
Future Market Insights (business website), 29

Glassdoor (employment website), 43, 44

Harrison, Glenn, 48, 49
Hermé, Pierre, 6–7
Hillson, Lee, 4–5
Hodges, Cyd Mitchell, 9

International Alliance of Theatrical Stage Employees, 43
International Association of Culinary Professionals (IACP), 45
Iron Chef America (TV program), 4

Joyce, Jennifer, 44

Kadoya, Soichi, 57–58
Khandelwal, Mallika, 47
Kilcoyne, Kevin, 17
knives (*hocho*), 15, 17, 20, 58

Lang, Jon, 48
Larousse Gastronomique, 30
Long, Brett, 41–42

Markoff, Katrina, 22
Master Brewers Certificate Program (University of California, Davis), 51
Master of Japanese Cuisine Academy, 18, 21
McQuaid, Peter, 33
McWhorter, Lance, 35
Medina, Katie, 9–10
mentorships, 32–33, 45
microbreweries, 47
Morgan, Haydon, 46

National Restaurant Association, 18, 45

Occupational Outlook Handbook (Bureau of Labor Statistics), 59
Oliver, Chris, 41
Ono, Jiro, 19

pastry chef
  education/training requirements for, 6, 8–9
  employers of, 11
  future job outlook for, 6, 13
  information on, 13
  internships, 8–9
  number of jobs for, 6
  role of, 6–8
  salary/earnings for, 6, 12
  skills/personal qualities of, 6, 11
  working conditions for, 6, 11–12
Pastry Chefs of America, 13
Peters, Christina, 38, 40

Ransom, Warren, 15, 16, 18
Research Chefs Association (RCA), 37
Retail Bakers of America, 13

Sakuta, Yoshio, 17
Salary.com (job evaluation site), 12
sashimi, 14
Schimmel, Mark, 24
Scott, Elle Simone, 41
ServSafe training (National Restaurant Association), 18

Siebel Institute of Technology, 50
Smith, Chris, 35
Spychala, Lisa, 40
Strain, Tae, 33
Sushi Chef Institute (SCI), 21
sushi chef (*itamae*), **19**
certification, 18
education/training requirements for, 14, 16–18
employers of, 19–20
future job outlook for, 14, 21
information on, 21
interview with, 57–58
number of jobs for, 14
role of, 14–16
salary/earnings for, 14, 20
skills/personal qualities of, 14, 18
working conditions for, 14, 20
Sydney Cove (ship), 46

technical brewer, 48
Thibert, Ceridwyn, 52
Tracy, Estelle, 23

University of California, Davis, 51

wakita (apprentice sushi chef), 17
White, Stephanie, 31, 35
Willis, Brooke, 28
World Association of Chef Societies, 37
World Brewing Academy (WBA), 50

Zippia (career website), 20
ZipRecruiter (employment website), 28

Picture Credits

Cover: Anel Alijagic/Shutterstock

10: David Herraez Calzada/Shutterstock
19: Shakirov Albert/Shutterstock
26: Carlo Prearo/Shutterstock
34: ZUMA Press/Alamy Stock Photo
43: Shutterstock.com
50: FXQuadro/Shutterstock

About the Author

Stuart A. Kallen is the author of more than 350 nonfiction books for children and young adults. He has written on topics ranging from the theory of relativity to the art of electronic dance music. In 2018, Kallen won a Green Earth book award from the Nature Generation environmental organization. He has also written award-winning children's videos and TV scripts. In his spare time, he is a singer, songwriter, and guitarist in San Diego.